ST. NICHOLAS
THE WONDER WORKER

ST. NICHOLAS
THE WONDER WORKER

Anne E. Neuberger

Our Sunday Visitor Publishing Division
Our Sunday Visitor, Inc.
Huntington, Indiana 46750

ISBN: 0-87973-481-7
LCCCN: 00-130462

Cover design by Monica Haneline
Cover and text illustrations by Tessie Bundick
PRINTED IN THE UNITED STATES OF AMERICA

Dedicated . . .

to my parents, Loretta and Edward Neuberger,

who first introduced me to St. Nicholas;

to Paul, who celebrates St. Nicholas Day

with me each year;

and to our Nicholas, our blessing,

who always surprises us!

The author would like to thank the many
people who have generously given
assistance in the making of this book and
shared enthusiasm for St. Nicholas,
especially Dennis Engleman
and Bill Phillips.

Contents

Introduction

It was December fifth. The kitchen was warm with light, the smells of the dinner just finished, and the watery sounds of dishes being washed. In the rest of the small house, it was dark, as December nights are meant to be. None of the life in the kitchen attracted me, however. I was straining to listen for another sound. I had been waiting, longing all afternoon, and now that it was evening, I knew it would come soon.

Bang!

That was the back door. Heart pounding, I skidded through the kitchen, threw open the door, and there it was: the bag of candy. St. Nicholas had come yet another year!

But this time, I was not content to leave it just at candy, as delightful as the anticipation was, and as delicious as the candy would be. I wanted to see St. Nicholas himself.

I peered around. He was no longer in our garage, which seemed painfully ordinary for a place that had so recently hosted St. Nicholas! Dashing back into the house, I rushed to my bedroom window. Snow drifted down, glistening in the arc of white light thrown by the streetlamp. I peered closely to see if there were footprints left by the good man. None were discernible from the regular traffic of the day.

I did not exactly know whom I was looking for. Having seen pictures of St. Francis, but none of St. Nicholas, I wondered if Nicholas might be dressed like Francis. But there was no one about. He was already gone.

I have not been contented ever since, though to this day I still enjoy the special kind of chocolate candy I relished later that night. Throughout the years, I have wondered about St. Nicholas. Even as an adult, I have felt a kind of pull, an urging, to follow him through the snow and find out who he is.

While I came to understand the ways of gift giving, I never stopped believing in St. Nicholas. Instead of looking out the window for the man, I have been looking for ways to find the spirit, looking for a way to keep on believing.

Why? Because I refuse to accept that the spirit of giving and delight is made up. I can't believe that this all-loving and all-knowing being who cares about me is a fabrication.

Many parents choose to tell their children of Santa Claus, the

Tooth Fairy, an Easter Bunny. They do this to convey this giving spirit. This anticipation, this delight, brings a sweetness to life that is irreplaceable. But there is more: when a child believes in an unseen someone who is all-loving, all-giving, all-knowing, then the seed has been planted for that child to know an all-loving, all-giving, all-knowing God we cannot see.

For some families, stories of Santa Claus, his North Pole residence, and chimney sliding bring much pleasure. Others find the image of the American Santa tarnished by commercialism, or are bothered by Santa's easy accessibility in public places, robbing him of his mystery.

In my quest for St. Nicholas, I have found Santa's ancestor, for that is one of St. Nicholas's many roles. And St. Nicholas, first as a man and then as a spirit, is a figure so powerful, so generous, and so mysterious, that he rivals even the one who lives at the North Pole and drives magic reindeer.

I could not go out into the snowy night and follow the St. Nicholas of my childhood. But I have pursued him now to offer this book to families searching for a gift-giving saint to believe in. Perhaps in reading these stories, families that are dissatisfied with Santa Claus will find they have all they need in St. Nicholas. They can begin celebrating his spirit, forming their own traditions. For those readers whose love lies with that generous, jolly man at the North Pole, these stories give him a past filled with great dignity.

What follows are stories of Nicholas for children and adults to share. We begin with those of his remarkable and long life, then follow with tales of miracles attributed to him after his death, as well as traditions that sprang up in many parts of the world in celebration of Nicholas. They can be used in the home, as nightly Advent reading, or in a classroom or perhaps in parish settings. The material introducing each story gives adult readers factual information, while the accompanying tale revolving around Nicholas's life is fictionalized and designed to be read aloud with children.

In writing this book, I have come to know St. Nicholas better now. (He does not dress like St. Francis, having lived centuries before!) Still, after all I've learned, he continues to leave for me a gift of the mysterious, the holy, the mystical, as he left chocolate on a long-ago December night.

It is my hope that in the darkness of a December night — as Advent slowly and gently brings us closer to the birth of the Christ

Child, and these stories are shared with one shining-eyed child or with a community of wiggly listeners — you will find the spirit of St. Nicholas alive and well, in history, in legend, in custom, and in yourselves.

Part I

The Life of Nicholas the Bishop

1

A Miracle Baby

Nicholas was born in the busy port town of Patara, Asia Minor (southeast Turkey), around the year 280. Christianity was a minor religion during those years of the Roman Empire. Nicholas's parents, well-to-do merchants, were members of a small Christian community that may have been founded by St. Paul years before.

"He is a miracle," said Theophane. "He is a gift from God!"

He looked down at the tiny baby in his arms, tears filling his eyes. "He is our miracle," he murmured.

From her bed his wife, Nonna, smiled. All these years she had waited, had hoped, had prayed, that God would give them a baby. Now, she had been blessed with a son! She treasured this sight of her beloved husband holding their newborn child. The baby was truly a miracle, being born to parents so old. What a blessing!

"We name you Nicholas," said Theophane to the baby. "We shall name you after your uncle."

"Perhaps one day, you will become a priest like him," said Nonna, her eyes never leaving the child's perfect face.

Theophane turned to Nonna. "The Lord has looked upon us, like Abraham and Sarah, and Elizabeth and Zechariah long ago. Their sons became very great men."

Nonna smiled.

The nurse attending her said softly, "We should bathe the child, sir."

Theophane nodded, reluctantly handing the baby to her. A warm bath had been prepared for the newborn. The nurse expertly lowered the tiny infant in, and then gasped.

This baby, just minutes old, was standing up! And he was holding his hands to heaven, as if in prayer!

The nurse cried out. Theophane and Nonna stared, then looked at each other.

"A miracle," Nonna murmured.

"I have delivered many babies," said the nurse. "Never, never have I seen this!"

Theophane knelt down beside his son and took the baby's rosebud hand into his.

"What will become of a child with such beginnings?" he asked.

2

A Healing Touch

Nonna and Theophane provided their son with a good education. Young Nicholas liked to study, and learned the Scriptures particularly well. Some say he began performing miracles while he was still a boy.

"Only goodness and kindness follow all the days of my life; and I shall dwell in the house of the Lord for years to come."

The child's voice, clear and sweet, filled the room.

"And which psalm is that?" Nonna asked.

"Psalm 23," Nicholas answered promptly.

Nicholas was seven years old now, and his schooling had begun in earnest. Theophane and Nonna wanted the best education for their son. Nonna taught him the Holy Scriptures herself.

Theophane entered the room, smiling at the sight of mother and child in study.

"I am going to church now," Theophane said. "Coming, Nicholas?"

"Yes, Father!"

Nonna's eyes met her husband's. They always marveled at Nicholas's love of Scripture and his desire to pray regularly.

It was a fine morning as the father and son walked through the streets of Patara. The smell of the sea filled the air, and the sun cast diamonds of light on the great waters. In the distance, they could see a ship leaving the harbor.

"Later today, we must visit a family whose home burned down. They're staying with relatives, but they have very little. Your mother learned of them yesterday. We'll take them food and clothing, and see if they are in need of money also," Theophane said.

Nicholas nodded. He had accompanied both of his parents often on such errands. Throughout Patara, they were known and loved for their generosity. Nicholas took it for granted.

Theophane noticed a woman walking toward them. He did not know her but had seen her before. She carried her left hand limply at her side, as she struggled with a heavy bundle with her right.

"We should help her," Nicholas said.

Before Theophane could reply, the woman hurried up to them. Quickly, she knelt down before them.

Nicholas drew back. Theophane, greatly troubled, asked, "Can I help you?"

"Please, let the child touch my hand," she whispered. With her good arm, she held up the withered, limp hand toward Nicholas. "I have heard that he is a special child. Maybe it will help, if he would touch it."

Nicholas looked uncertainly at his father. Theophane drew in a deep breath, taking in the significance of her request. He hesitated. But perhaps this was what God wanted. . . .

"Go ahead, Nicholas," Theophane said softly.

The child stretched out his small smooth hand and touched hers.

She cried out, "Oh! Oh, I feel warmth! I feel life in it! Thank you, thank you! You are indeed a most special child! Thank you!"

The woman hurried down the street, waving her hand like a freedom flag.

Nicholas and his father watched her go, then walked on. Neither spoke.

What, wondered Theophane, would become of this wondrous child?

3
Gold in the Night

Nicholas's happy childhood came to a sudden end when an epidemic swept through Patara. The illness killed many, including Nicholas's beloved parents, Nonna and Theophane. Nicholas was a teenager, and plans for his immediate future were made; but first, Nicholas wanted to give away his inheritance. It was then that he began a practice that would cause him to be remembered for centuries: giving to others in secret, often in the dark hours of the night.

"This is a tremendous loss. There are many people of Patara indebted to your parents' kindness. Theophane and Nonna were remarkable in their ways, as you know. I will miss them greatly, too, but I can't compare my grief to yours. To lose both parents, at your young age, Nicholas, is truly a tragedy. I am deeply sorry," Uncle Nicholas said gently.

Fifteen-year-old Nicholas nodded. "Thank you," he answered, "but there's grief everywhere. The illness that took my parents killed many others, too."

For a moment there was silence, until the uncle ventured, "Do you want to discuss your future now?"

"Yes," Nicholas said. "I'd like to join your monastery. I have always known I would become a priest someday."

His uncle smiled. "That was your parents' greatest hope, from the time you were born."

"I want a life of solitude and prayer."

"You are very young, but I'll arrange it. I think you will be a wonderful priest. Certainly you cannot stay here, so after things are settled here, you may join me."

"There's much to be taken care of," Nicholas said,

knowing his father's business affairs and his own inherited wealth were considerable.

"Your inheritance cannot come with you, you know," his uncle said.

"I understand," Nicholas replied. He had already begun to give his money away.

"Well, now," Uncle Nicholas said, standing up to leave. "I've no doubt that the son of Nonna and Theophane will find a good use for that money. We will speak again soon."

When his uncle had gone, the loneliness of the house and his life echoed throughout his feelings of emptiness. Nicholas was relieved to have a direction, and he was glad to learn that his beloved parents would have been in agreement with his plans.

In this sad time, there was one merriment. Nicholas was taking great delight in giving his money away. When he saw someone in need, he would leave money or a gift without being seen, for Jesus had instructed his disciples to give to others without boasting. For Nicholas, this meant giving in secret. Sneaking about at night on a mysterious mission was great fun!

On the night he had talked with his uncle, Nicholas made plans for yet another late-night adventure. He knew that his neighbor, a nobleman, had lost all his money through bad luck and bad judgment. This meant the man's three daughters had no dowries, which were sums of money to bring to their marriages. Without a dowry, there could be no marriage. Without marriages, these young women were doomed — doomed to lives of slavery! When he heard rumors of the girls' fate, Nicholas had known what to do. His uncle's instructions to give away his inheritance only strengthened his plans.

Slipping on a long cloak, he pulled the hood up to

conceal his face. Out in the street, he walked carefully, staying close to houses, running when he thought no one was about. Once, he heard someone leave a nearby home. Nicholas stepped into the shadows, hoping his rapid breathing would not give him away. When the footsteps that had caused him to hide faded away, he moved back into the street, running again.

The bag of gold felt cold and heavy in his hand, but Nicholas knew it meant freedom for the oldest daughter. He hesitated a moment, looking the house over. He chose a window. Stealthily he dropped the bag. *Thud!* Smiling, he hurried away, again keeping to the shadows.

Within days, there was talk among the neighbors. Had the nobleman's luck changed? It seemed there were plans for his oldest daughter to be wed! Nicholas smiled, but he said nothing.

He did not want to leave the girl's two sisters in despair. Another moonless night arrived. He again pulled on the long cloak. As before, he slunk from his house to the neighbors'. Unsuspecting that such generosity should come again, the family slept, never hearing the bag of gold hit the floor.

And the second daughter was wed.

That left the last sister. Nicholas sneaked out as before, cloak swinging. He did not know the grateful father was waiting for him.

Slipping the bag through the window, he waited for the soft thud, but instead he heard a scrambling in the house and a door opening. He did not wait to hear more.

Running madly in the darkness, Nicholas strove to lose his pursuer. The father, determined to thank him, was relentless. Through the streets of Patara, in the dead of the night, ran the two men. Finally, the father caught Nicholas.

"Why, it's young Nicholas!" the panting father marveled. "Oh, dear neighbor! And you who have recently lost so much! How can I ever thank you enough for your gifts? You have saved my daughters! I will be forever grateful to you!"

Then, falling to his knees, he bowed to Nicholas.

"Please, good sir, get up!" Nicholas urged in a whisper. "There is no need for this!"

But the father, remaining at Nicholas's feet, replied: "Without your help, my family would be ruined. I can never thank you enough!"

"Please!" Nicholas pleaded. "Please, get up!"

When the man stood, Nicholas went on, "Promise me something."

"Anything!"

"Promise me that you will never tell anyone that I gave you the money."

"Well, if that is how you want it — " the father began.

"Yes," Nicholas said briskly. "That is how I want it. It's all I ask."

"I promise, but please accept my gratitude, kind sir!"

Nicholas smiled and nodded.

"My daughters will be forever grateful!"

"Remember your promise," Nicholas said, and pulling his cloak around him, he disappeared into the shadows of the night.

4

The Boy Bishop

*Nicholas joined his uncle's monastery. After much study he was or-
dained a priest while still a very young man. With his uncle's permission, he then traveled to the Holy Land to see where Jesus had
lived and died three hundred years before. On the return voyage,
with his mind revolving around plans of a life of solitude and study,
his ship — and his life — were blown onto another course.*

Ships had always been part of Nicholas's life. As a
small boy in Patara, he watched merchant ships gracefully
come and go in the harbor. Now he stood alone aboard one
bound also for Patara. After months in the Holy Land,
Nicholas was coming home, back to the monastery, to begin
his adult life of prayer and solitude.

The trip there was uneventful, and the first half of this
return voyage had been calm, too. But now, that was
changing, fast. Ominous clouds began to gather on the
horizon.

"I don't like the look of this," the captain said, and
started shouting orders to the sailors to ready the ship for
the worst.

The winds began to rise, and soon the little ship was
buffeted and thrashed about in a storm. Two days and two
nights passed, but who could tell day from night? Waves
crashed and rolled over the railings. The terrified sailors
could do very little to save their passengers, their ship, or
themselves.

Frightened, Nicholas did what he could do: he prayed.
Soon the sailors joined him.

Before dawn of the third day, the storm began to subside.

"We survived," a bewhiskered sailor said. "And we have that young priest to thank. It was his prayers that saw us through."

"It was his prayers that stopped the storm!" another declared.

There were murmurs of agreement among the sailors. Nicholas responded only that he would give thanks in the nearest church.

But where had this storm taken them? By dawn they knew: in sight was Myra, the capital city, only twenty miles east of Patara!

The battered ship limped into the harbor, but it was a jubilant crew that rode in on her. Nicholas, too, rejoiced as he saw the shores of Myra coming closer.

Oh, how good it felt to have the solid, steady earth beneath his feet once again! Nicholas took a moment just to stand still. Then, in the early dawn hours, he began to walk in search of the church. As he threaded his way through the still-dark streets, he did not know that soon this would be home. Nor did he know that once he entered the church, his life would be forever changed.

Nicholas had been gone for months, so he did not know that the bishop of Myra had retired. During this time, the other bishops were meeting to select a new leader. So far, they had not agreed on anyone.

But just yesterday, the oldest member had a vision. In a dream, an angel told him how to choose the next bishop of Myra! It was an unusual procedure, but then, would an angel bring an ordinary message?

They were to go to the church, early in the morning, before the first light touched the sky. There they were to wait in the hallway, outside the main door of the church. The angel said that whoever entered the door first that morning would be a man worthy of the office.

"His name is Nicholas," the angel said.

So, as the unsuspecting Nicholas made his way to the church, the bishops, this group of elders, gathered in the shadows of the church hallway. Curious and excited, they waited, and waited, and waited.

Still rumpled from his stormy travels, Nicholas bounded up the steps and opened the door to the church. He was greeted by an assembly of expectant faces.

"Good morning," the oldest bishop said. "Excuse me, but what is your name?"

Nicholas looked about him, startled at this attention, but he answered politely, "I am Nicholas of Patara, your respectful servant."

"Praise God!" someone whispered.

"Then welcome, Father Nicholas," the same bishop said. "You have been chosen to be the next bishop of Myra."

Bishop! Nicholas stared at these people in the dark hallway. They smiled, as if all this made sense. But Nicholas was barely a priest, a young one at that. He could not become bishop!

Quickly, the vision was explained to him.

Still, Nicholas protested, "I am much too young!"

That did not matter. After all, he had been chosen. There was never any question in the minds of the others.

A ceremony was held. The studious child of Patara was now the bishop of Myra. A quiet life was not to be Nicholas's fate.

5

Saint in a Storm

The boy bishop grew into his role, learning the work of a bishop. Among his duties was his attendance at the Council of Nicaea, the first general council of the Christian Church. He was greatly loved and respected for his kindness, his generous giving, his deep faith, and his compassion for the poor and oppressed. But he also acquired a reputation for giving people assistance in another, and most unusual, way.

The sea rocked them gently that night, a night strewn with stars, a night kissed with gentle, warm breezes. The sailors not on duty were reluctant to go down to their stuffy quarters. Instead, they sat together on an open deck, singing songs, talking of home, and finally, telling stories.

Hali listened intently. It was stories like these, stories he heard as he sat on his grandfather's knee, that had called him to the sea. This was his first voyage. A night like this was what he had longed for.

The stories ranged from shipwrecks to differing ports, until one older sailor, Gorka, said, "Ever hear of the bishop of Myra, in Asia Minor? Name of Nicholas?"

There were many enthusiastic nods.

"Heard of him? My brother worked a ship he sailed on," another said. "He saw with his own eyes a miracle Nicholas performed!"

"Tell us!" Hali urged.

"One sailor was working up high, on the highest mast, when he slipped."

There was silence. Every sailor knew that fear.

"What happened?" Hali ventured.

"Well, he was killed, of course. Can't survive a fall from that high," the sailor said. "But someone called the bishop to come. You know, to say a prayer over the dead. But, as the bishop prayed, my brother said he looked, and looked again. The dead man was moving, just slightly, but he was moving! Soon he opened his eyes, then he sat up! He was sore, but alive! And, I tell you, he had been dead, minutes before!"

A few low whistles and murmurs of awe and admiration ended that story. Hali pulled closer to the circle.

"Well, I have heard other stories that Bishop Nicholas was on board a ship in a storm and stopped the storm by praying," Gorka said.

He rubbed his beard and looked out to sea, as if he could see the bishop as he spoke.

"I have another story," said a sailor who had been silent all the while. "I have been told this story by different sailors, all who were there. They served on a ship with an evil, greedy captain. Nicholas was on board this ship, and everyone could see what an exceptional person he was. Well, so could this captain. He decided not to take them to Asia Minor, where Nicholas was bound, but to stop someplace where he could sell Nicholas as a slave!"

There was a general muttering and grumbling against the captain among the listeners.

"As the story goes," the speaker continued, "Nicholas began praying, just like you said he did. But instead of stopping a storm, it seems he caused one. For a heavy wind came up, when there hadn't been much of one before, and lasted so long, that they were blown to the waters of Asia Minor against the captain's will."

Hali sat in silence, heavy with amazement and respect.

Gorka stood up, stretched his long arms, and said, "Well, may Nicholas hold the tiller! It's late, we'd better sleep."

The young sailor, however, lay awake, stories swirling in his head.

A few days later, the gentleness of that night seemed like another world to Hali. He woke to a greenish sky, with threatening clouds racing across it like terrified horses.

The sailors worked feverishly to ready the ship. Frightened and uncertain of his duties, Hali stayed close to Gorka.

Within minutes, a driving rain was upon them. The waves became vicious, as if some monstrous serpent was under the water, stirring them up. Panic was spreading through the sailors' ranks; some of them cried out, as if in pain. With the ship pitching and tossing, Hali clung to the railings, afraid that if he let go, he would be washed overboard.

He knew all was lost. The looks on the faces of the more experienced sailors told him so. He remembered other terrified sailors, the ones in the stories, and Hali shouted, "Let's pray to Nicholas!"

They prayed, prayed for their lives.

Immediately, there appeared a figure, in bishop's clothing! From nowhere it had come, but now it spoke, "You have called me. Here I am! There is more we can do."

They stared in disbelief, but now the figure began instructing the sailors. Soon they were working with him with sails and ropes and riggings. As they did so, the storm lessened. When it seemed safe enough to pause to thank the mysterious helper, he was gone.

They all agreed what they must do. As soon as

possible, the sailors headed to Myra. Finding the church where the bishop worked, they went in to pray. A tall man came into the church.

Hali stared at him. Gorka studied him. The others did, too. They knew who he was. He was the man in the vision, the one who had come to them in the storm. This was Bishop Nicholas! But this time, he was not a vision, but a real person.

The bishop listened intently to their story of the storm, the vision, and of his help.

"Thank you! We owe you our very lives!" Gorka said.

The tall bishop smiled, but said, "It is not me you should thank. Thank God, whose mercy saved you. And your faith!"

Then he smiled again, and left them, not mysteriously, but down a hallway and out a door, leaving the grateful sailors the quiet of the church in which to pray.

6

Grains of Justice

Bishop Nicholas was admired for his strong stands for justice and his unshakable belief in Jesus. When the emperor of the Roman Empire was Diocletian, around the year 303, all Christians were in danger of being imprisoned because of their religion. Nicholas was jailed for five years. After his release, he continued to live and fight for what he believed.

"My good man," said the tall man dressed in bishop's finery. "I ask only a hundred measures from each ship!"

The autumn wind pulled and tugged at his cloak, but the bishop stood his ground firmly.

"I'd like to help you, Bishop," the captain replied. "I really would. But I dare not. You see, our ships carry wheat that was carefully measured before we left Alexandria. We must take this — the entire load — to the emperor's granaries."

The sea lapped at these ships of plenty, splashed onto battered docks, in its ceaseless movement.

"There has been a great famine here in Myra. People are hungry," the bishop responded. "Yet you will deliver all this grain to a place where food is abundant?"

"I'm very sorry to hear of your misfortune, but the grain is not mine to give," the captain said.

"Winter comes soon," the bishop went on, "and people will starve. Is this justice, that some suffer while others feast?"

"I wish I could help you," the captain said, almost wistfully.

"I ask only a hundred measures from each ship," the

bishop repeated. "Do as I say. Through God's power, you will not find the wheat short at your journey's end."

The captain gazed at the bishop. This was a crazy idea, of course, but there was something about this man that made the captain believe him, made him trust when there was no sense to it.

"All right." Then turning to his crew, the captain shouted, "One hundred measures is to be taken from each ship!"

The grain was unloaded, the ships once again began their journey. But something much greater had begun.

When the ships arrived at their destination and were weighed, nothing was found amiss. The hundred measures in each ship had been refilled, just as Nicholas had promised. The captain and sailors began praising the God they now knew through Nicholas. Everywhere they traveled, each time they journeyed afar, they told others of the dignified bishop of Myra who taught them of God's tremendous power.

In Myra, the bishop divided the grain among the many hungry people. The small portions miraculously lasted two full years, feeding all who needed the grain, but there was also enough left over for planting. Memories of the bishop's miracles were told to children and grandchildren.

Stories of Nicholas had begun to spread.

7
A Man of Action

Nicholas lived during the era of the Roman Empire. As a public fig-ure, Nicholas's work was affected by this government, and he en-countered Roman officials with varying levels of authority. In the following story, he graciously entertains three visiting Roman gen-erals. However, when the local Roman consul commits a crime, these generals see that Nicholas, gentle and humble as a dove, could turn into a lion.

"It's kind of you to invite us, since we arrived so unexpectedly," the Roman general Nepotian said to Bishop Nicholas as they sat at the table.

Ursus and Apilion, his fellow generals, agreed. They looked with curiosity at this bishop, who was smiling so gently and warmly at them.

"I understand your situation," Nicholas replied. "I've been in storms at sea myself."

"When the winds picked up, we thought it was wisest to stop in Myra for the time being. We hope to be on our way soon," said Ursus.

Nicholas nodded. "Well, I hope you enjoy your stay here. I must tell you that I invited you here to ask something, and hope you can understand my situation."

The three generals listened. They liked this bishop, who despite his honors, had a manner of humbleness like that of a child.

"When ships such as yours come into port, it is common that the crew members come into town on market day. The townspeople tell me much stealing happens those days. I do not wish to accuse your men, sirs. Please, do not misunderstand me. If you think your crew might be stealing, I ask only that you take steps to prevent it."

There was a knock at the door, and an excited man entered the room without waiting for permission. He went straight to the bishop.

"Good bishop, excuse my interruption, but I must speak now! Time is running out!" he cried.

"Speak," Nicholas replied.

"The Roman consul has accepted a bribe, one that means that three innocent soldiers have been sentenced to death! Because it was a bribe, he wants the sentences carried out immediately. As we speak, the men are being prepared! I have proof that they are innocent, but only you can stop their deaths now!"

Nicholas stood up. "Come with me!"

The three generals left the comfort of the table and followed Nicholas and the distraught man out the door. Nicholas was calm, but he moved with great speed. In minutes, they saw an executioner, with sword in hand. Three terrified soldiers awaited his violence. The executioner raised his arms.

The bishop hurled himself at the man with the sword and both fell to the ground, Nicholas grabbing the sword from the other's hand.

"They will not die," Nicholas declared loudly into the face of the executioner. Then catching his breath, he stood up and said to the man he had come with, "Take these men to safety. I will deal with other matters."

Not bothering to brush himself off, the bishop began to walk swiftly again, calling back to the three astonished generals, "You are welcome to come along!"

Again, they hurried after the bishop down the streets of Myra until they reached the headquarters of the Roman consul, the person who had taken the bribe and ordered the punishments of the three soldiers.

The door was locked. Nicholas threw his full weight at it, but the door did not open.

The generals offered their help, and together, they forced the door open. As soon as it swung open, the consul came scurrying into the room.

"Bishop! It is an honor to have you come!" he said nervously, looking from bishop to generals. "I was coming to open the door. I did not know you were coming or I would have — "

"You enemy of God!" Nicholas roared. "How dare you look us in the eye when you've such a crime on your conscience!"

And he did not stop there. The generals watched and listened. The once gentle bishop continued to shout reproaches at the consul, who stood looking very much like a condemned man himself. Nicholas's voice filled the room, filled their souls.

Finally, Nepotian urged Nicholas to stop. The consul was on his knees now, crying and begging forgiveness. Taking a deep breath, Nicholas gave the consul a blessing.

The winds died down soon after this, and the three generals were able to continue their travels. But as their ship slipped from the harbor, they knew they would not soon forget the powerful bishop of Myra.

8

The Emperor's Dream

The emperor Constantine was a powerful man, and one who did many great things for Christianity. But the bishop Nicholas was also very powerful, a Christian who worked for those who were powerless.

Constantine, the great Roman emperor, was sleeping.

In the prison, however, three of his generals — Nepotian, Ursus, and Apilion — were not sleeping, could not sleep. Just that day, they had been arrested and told there would be no trial. Soon, very soon, they would die.

They had done nothing wrong. In fact, they had done a particularly good job and had previously been honored by the emperor. Others, jealous of these generals' honors, had made up stories about them, convincing Emperor Constantine and his administrator that the three generals deserved to be sentenced to death.

No, they did not sleep. They talked quietly, fearfully.

"Do you remember when we were in Myra?" Nepotian said suddenly. "Do you remember the bishop there?"

"Of course," answered Ursus. "How could I forget Nicholas?"

"I wish he were here now, to save us as he saved those three innocent soldiers!" Apilion lamented.

"Let's pray! Let's pray that somehow Nicholas can help us here," Nepotian said.

The others agreed. Dying men need some hope, however unlikely it may seem.

While the condemned men prayed, the emperor slept.

He did not sleep well, however. He had a disturbing dream. A man, dressed in bishop's clothing, appeared to the emperor. This bishop said, "Why did you have the generals arrested unjustly? Why would you have them die when they are innocent? Hurry! Get up! See to it that they are set free at once or you will regret it!"

Being emperor, Constantine was not used to people talking this way to him, not even in a dream. Still dreaming, the emperor asked, "Who are you to talk to me this way?"

"I am Nicholas, bishop of Myra," came the answer.

Constantine woke up.

At the same time, in another room, the administrator was sleeping. He, too, was having a restless night. A bishop had appeared to him in a dream.

"Senseless man! Why did you agree to punishing innocent men? Get up! Go at once and see to it that they are set free! If you do not, you will regret it!"

In his dream, the man asked, "Who are you to threaten me so?"

"Know that I am Nicholas, bishop of the city of Myra," came the reply, and the dream ended.

The administrator sat up, shaking. What could this mean? Did he dare wake the emperor for a dream? Should he have the men freed? Before he decided, there was a knock at the door. He was to come at once to the emperor.

The two men discussed their dreams, and the emperor had the three prisoners sent for. When they stood before him, Constantine said, "We had dreams about you. Are you magicians? How did you give us such visions?"

Nepotian answered respectfully that they were not magicians, nor had they done anything wrong to deserve this sentence.

The emperor asked, "Do you know a man, a bishop, named Nicholas?"

The three generals looked at one another, amazed. All three then raised their hands in prayer, asking God to save them from this fate.

The emperor listened as they prayed, then asked them to tell him all they knew about the bishop. When they finished, Constantine dismissed them, saying, "Go and thank God who has saved you through this Nicholas. But then, go to Myra, bring gifts in my name to the bishop. Ask him to pray for me and my reign."

The three generals, happy, free people, traveled to Myra, where they met once more with Bishop Nicholas. They explained their story of imprisonment, prayer, and dreams to him.

"We knew you were a good man when we were first here, but now we know that you are a servant of God!" Nepotian said.

The bishop listened intently, then raised his hands to heaven. Turning back to the generals, he said, "My good men, sit down. I have much to tell you of this God's tremendous love and power."

Conclusion of Part I

Nicholas had lived a long, full life. When he was very old, he knew God was calling him again, this time for a life of the spirit. It was December 6, 343, when Nicholas said his last words, "In the Lord I put my trust."

Many mourned his death, for Nicholas was greatly loved, as his parents had been before him. His body was buried in a marble tomb. Soon, a remarkable liquid began flowing from this tomb. Small drops of it could cure illnesses. It was called Holy Myro, for this liquid was like myrrh. People came from all around to visit the tomb, and to be cured by the liquid. Containers of it were taken far from Myra. These pilgrims also took with them stories of St. Nicholas, and a love for him that would spread over many countries, and over many centuries.

The life of Nicholas the Bishop was over, but the life of Nicholas the Spirit has just begun.

Part II

The Life of Nicholas the Spirit

Introduction to Part II

For seven hundred years after Nicholas's death, proof of his miracles was recorded. Stories of the appearance of St. Nicholas in times of need, of lost children found and sick people cured through his intercession, of customs based on the life of Nicholas — all these stories are present in many European cultures. Countries such as Russia, Greece, Germany, Austria, Belgium, France, the Netherlands, and Sicily claimed him as patron, as did the cities of Liège, Lucerne, Freiburg, Amsterdam, and Aberdeen. He became patron to sailors, weavers, bakers, children, travelers, bankers, unmarried girls, pawnbrokers, schoolboys, and even thieves. At one time, some two thousand churches, hospitals, and monasteries were named for him, with sixty churches in Rome alone. By the end of the 1400s, St. Nicholas was considered the third most beloved religious figure, after Christ and Mary.

Few figures of history have had their life stories as woven into custom and enjoyment as Nicholas of Myra. Tales of Nicholas's influence go on and on, right up to the present day. The following stories tell of some of his miracles, and of traditions that grew from Nicholas's inspiration, from the days in Turkey some years after Nicholas's death, to today, where his spirit still lives on.

9

A Tale from Turkey: The Rescue of the Fisherman's Son

The miracles of St. Nicholas were recognized even before his death, and one particular story gave him the status of "protector of children." Three boys were killed and their bodies were placed in brine by a wicked innkeeper. When visiting the inn, Bishop Nicholas suspected something was wrong. Discovering this atrocity, he brought the boys back to life. Other stories, mainly ones after Nicholas's death, also tell of his saving children. One of these stories, probably from the time shortly after Nicholas died, is a less grisly tale, and shows the saint's love of children.

Basil skipped and bounced along the water's edge, daring the small waves to catch him and wet his toes. The rhythmic sound of the waves coming to shore was as much a part of Basil's life as the air he breathed. One wave, a bit larger than the others, caught him by surprise, splashing his feet and legs up to his knees.

The boy laughed into the wind.

"You won that time!" he said to the sea. "But you can't catch me again!"

With that, Basil danced and twirled as he headed down the shore, dodging the waves and looking out toward the sea where his father was fishing. Often Basil waited for his father's return, dreaming of the day when he would be old enough to work with his father.

But today, he had other thoughts. For it was the sixth of December, St. Nicholas Day. His parents had great devotion to the saint who had been bishop there many years before. They said he was a holy man, and they honored him, celebrating the memory of his life each year. At home, his mother was preparing a special meal. Soon, the family would pray, feast, and laugh together. This was one of the happiest days each year.

There was a strange ship anchored not far from where he played, but Basil lived near Myra, a busy port town, so new ships were not a curiosity. Once again, Basil peered out to the sea, looking for his father's boat. He never heard the two men who crept up behind him.

Strong arms went around him, a rough bag was pulled over his head, and Basil was carried off before he could even scream. On that part of the shore, no one but the two kidnappers were there to hear anyway.

When he was released from the bag, Basil was horrified to find himself on the ship he had noticed earlier. The ship was moving, and his home was slipping away from him.

Basil's next year was filled with new sights and sounds, but never any happiness. Now he was a slave, a servant to the king in a country far from home. Each day, dressed in servant's clothing, he served the king his food. Basil's special job was holding the king's golden goblet.

Often he wondered about his parents. They would be sick with worry and sadness, he knew. He thought of St. Nicholas, of the feast day he never got to celebrate. One day, as he stood before the king, golden cup in hand, Basil realized a year had passed. It was St. Nicholas Day, again. How he longed to be home celebrating with his mother and father! Basil began to cry.

The king saw him, and laughed. "It does you no good to cry. You will never go home," he said.

Suddenly a wind filled the house. It grew stronger and

stronger, until the very walls began to tremble. Even the king was alarmed.

Basil was amazed when he felt hands on him, gentle but strong, then arms picking him up. He was being raised up, high above the palace!

"Do not be afraid, Basil," a voice said. "I am taking you home. Your parents prayed, asking that I bring you to them."

Basil turned to look into kind, loving eyes. He knew without asking that his rescuer was the good St. Nicholas.

In what seemed like moments, he was safely on the ground, though he knew not when he landed. The saint was gone, and a dog was barking. Basil stood in front of a gate, still dressed in servant's clothing, still holding the golden goblet. What had happened?

The dog kept barking. The dog! It was his dog! This was home!

"It's Basil!" he heard someone cry. "Come quickly! Basil, our Basil is home!"

Amid shouts, tears, and hugs, Basil's family welcomed him, carrying him into the house, where a St. Nicholas Day feast lay untouched on the table.

His parents were overjoyed and thankful, yet bewildered. After Basil told them of his kidnapping and his work as a servant, his mother pointed to the food on the table.

"We tried to celebrate without you, but our hearts were not in it. We could only pray for your safety," his mother said, stroking her child's cheeks. "How did you get here? How did you escape?"

Basil smiled. "I think, when I tell you, you will celebrate with all your heart."

10

A Tale from Italy:
To Walk Proudly

Because of the Holy Myro, the fragrant, healing liquid flowing from Nicholas's tomb, Myra became a place for people seeking miracles. But by the year 1087, non-Christians had taken over the city, making it difficult for the numerous pilgrims seeking the holy bishop's tomb. In Italy, many people believed in his sainthood; consequently, in the spring of that year, a fleet of Italian merchants sailing to Turkey decided to "rescue" the remains, and bring them to Italy, where a new tomb could be built. Some stories say they forced the monks in charge of the tomb to give them the bones. Others say the monks had dreamed that St. Nicholas had told them to allow the merchants to remove the bones. In any case, the arrival of the very precious bones in Bari, Italy, on May ninth, was a cause for great celebration. And it is recorded that on that day, forty-seven people were cured of illnesses, twenty-two were healed the second day, and twenty-nine the third day — all through the miraculous power of St. Nicholas.

Over the centuries, a three-day festival has become a tradition to commemorate this time. Huge numbers of pilgrims arrive on the eighth of May to pray at the cathedral, shuffling slowly over the flagstones on their knees. Emotions run high as some people faint while others speak in tongues. In the evening, an old Norman castle is floodlit, and drummers clad in medieval clothing lead a parade making its way by torchlight. At the end of this parade comes a replica of a sailing ship like the one that brought the remains of St. Nicholas, pulled by sailors and merchants. Early in the morning of May ninth, after Mass in the cathedral, a life-size statue of St. Nicholas is taken from the cathedral and processed through the town down to the sea, where the bishop blesses the waters with the Holy Myro. The statue is escorted back at nightfall, with fireworks and singing. The *final ceremony, on the tenth of May, is the gathering of the Holy Myro from the tomb. Many families bring their own containers, richly decorated bottles that have been handed down from generation to generation.*

"Hold still!" Nicia's mother insisted. "I can't comb your hair when you wiggle so. I have many things to do before we leave."

Nicia sighed and tried to cooperate. She was always dancing and leaping, running and jumping. She hated to hold still, especially to have her hair combed.

"Why do we have to go?"

"Have to go? We want to go! It is an honor to be part of it. There, all finished. Now, little bird, try not to mess your hair and do not get your dress dirty," Mama said, giving Nicia a little kiss on her forehead.

Grandmother, who had watched from her chair, called, "Nicia, come to me. I will tell you a story until it's time to go. Sit down, little fluttering bird!"

Nicia cuddled up to the comfortable warmth that was Grandmother. She could hold still for a story. "What is it about?"

In reply, her grandmother began:

It's about your great-grandfather, Paolo, and something wonderful that happened a long time ago. When he was very young, he had an accident, and after that, he could no longer walk. He had to be carried about, and sometimes his older brother Gian would put him in a little cart and push him where they needed to go.

One day — it was May ninth, just as it is today — Paolo was playing in the house when Gian came running in.

62

"Mama! Paolo! A ship has just arrived with a most precious cargo!" Gian called.

Paolo looked out the window and saw people hurrying past their house. Some were shouting; all were excited.

"What is it?" Mama asked.

"It's a ship returning from Turkey. The men aboard have brought back the remains of St. Nicholas! Of San Nicola!"

"Why?" Paolo asked.

"Myra has been overtaken by people who made it impossible for Christians to get to the tomb. So the men from here, from Bari, took the saint's precious bones, and brought them here."

Paolo saw his mother put her fingers to her cheeks in astonishment. In a whisper she asked, "San Nicola? Here? They will build a tomb here? What an honor!"

"Yes," Gian said impatiently. "People from all over the city are going to the harbor in welcome. Let's go! We don't want to be the last ones there!"

Then he looked at Paolo, whose crutch lay on the floor next to him. "Come, little brother, I will run with you in the cart."

Bump, bump, bump-bump! Paolo clung to the sides of the wagon that Gian pushed as he ran. The closer they drew to the harbor, the more crowded it became, and Paolo was jostled at every step. Finally they could see the ship.

"What is happening?" Paolo called to his mother. In the cart, he could not see anything but adults' legs and clothes.

"The men who brought the relics are bringing the chest down from the ship, the chest that contains the saint's remains," she answered. "This is such an honor,

63

Paolo! It is a great day! You'll remember this all your life!"

What was there to remember, wondered Paolo, but a fast ride and much noise? For singing had begun now, amid shouts of joy and cries of praise for the saint. Then the joy turned to anger. Paolo heard people argue, "Where are you taking the chest?"

"Not to the cathedral!"

"Take it to the monastery!"

On and on went the arguments until it was settled that, for the time being, the chest should rest at the monastery. A special church could be built later. Finally, it was being carried reverently through the crowds.

Paolo, who was a patient child, had had enough. "Mama, please, take me home!" he pleaded. How he wished he could run, run like the other children. He would be home already, playing.

But his mother was talking among the people near them.

"Just have him touch the chest," a woman next to his mother said. "I've heard there's a chance of a miracle. Someone up ahead said sick people were touching the chest in hopes of being cured."

The procession with the chest was coming their way.

"Come, Paolo," said his mother. She began pushing the cart, inching her way through the crowd. "I want you to touch the chest."

"I want to go home, Mama!"

"Hush," she said, but Paolo knew no one heard a whining child in this noise. She pushed relentlessly on until she was in sight of the men with the chest. "I've heard many stories that San Nicola works miracles.

Lean forward when they come near. Touch the chest," she insisted.

Paolo did as he was told, for the chest was pretty and he wanted to see how it felt. The men carrying it paused for him to reach out as they had for others in the crowd. Then they moved on.

"Mama!" Paolo shouted. "I feel funny. My legs, my legs feel like I can move them!"

Quickly his mother bent down to look. Paolo wiggled his legs, wiggled them again, and again. Then, slowly, he tried to stand up. He was unsteady at first, but then, yes, he could stand!

"It is a miracle! The lame walk! My child is cured!" his mother cried joyfully. People around him began shouting, praising, and blessing San Nicola.

"And what happened to Paolo?" Nicia asked.

"Paolo? He walked, he ran home! And he ran and played all year, until the next year on the ninth of May, when he walked proudly and strongly in the procession held in Bari to celebrate the anniversary of San Nicola's arrival."

Nicia's grandmother added, "Every year, he walked and sang in the great procession. He helped carry a large statue of the saint out to sea and back again. Every year, for his long, long life, Paolo participated. And when Paolo no longer walked in the procession, his children — my brother and I — we walked in it. And now my children and grandchild — you — walk in the procession. You, Nicia, who were named for San Nicola. And, now it is time to go."

Soon, Nicia watched as her father and other men entered the magnificent basilica and came out carrying the life-size statue of San Nicola. The many musicians, waiting for this moment, began a lively tune. Nicia ran to be with her father, and the procession began. As the men moved to the music, San Nicola swayed and dipped a little, on his yearly trip to the sea.

In every doorway, window, and alley, people crowded around to watch San Nicola pass. And Nicia, great-grandchild of Paolo, walked proudly down the streets of Bari.

11

A Tale from France: The Sweetness of Surprise

In many parts of the world, gift giving, in secret or with some element of surprise, is an important part of Christmas celebrations. Nicholas of Myra considered generosity and gift giving part of being Christian. That he gave anonymously was also based in his religious beliefs, for Christ taught to give alms in secret (Matthew 6:1-4.) However, it was not a well-kept secret, for it is that trait for which we most remember Nicholas, and his descendant, Santa Claus. His spirit of giving has remained strong throughout the centuries, working through many people in many lands. His love of giving in secret has inspired much delight and an array of traditions. Secretly leaving treats on the eve of St. Nicholas Day is thought to have originated in France, during the twelfth century, when a group of nuns were inspired to imitate Nicholas's gift-giving midnight missions.

The oranges gave a deep, fruity smell to the small room. Their warm color was a delightful sight on this dark winter night. Sister Maria Felicia looked over the bowls of nuts that lay in waiting, too. A stack of cheerfully colored cloth, cut into squares, brightened the table.

She took in a deep breath, holding in the aroma of the oranges, then sighed contentedly. This was a night for surprises!

A few weeks before, there had been talk in her convent of the good St. Nicholas, whose feast day was approaching. The Sisters were amused that local schoolboys were planning a "Boy Bishop" celebration, where the boys played at being bishop because St. Nicholas himself had been very young when appointed bishop. But the Sisters' conversation

69

had drifted to other ways Nicholas was remembered. His giving money in secret late at night to those in need was much admired.

That night, Sister Maria Felicia had been unable to sleep. Other children, not so fortunate as the schoolboys, kept coming to mind. She had seen them in the streets. The poor children, those with ragged clothing torn by the wind, those with hollow cheeks, and eyes that did not sparkle but instead looked out dully onto a cruel world — those she could not forget. Just before she finally fell asleep, she thought of St. Nicholas. And Sister Maria Felicia began to plan.

And now, it was time for that plan!

She heard the footsteps and soft voices of the other Sisters in the hallway. Soon the room was filled with happy workers.

Conversation and laughter mingled in the air as some Sisters sewed the cloth into bags, and others stuffed the bags with the oranges and nuts. Sister Maria Felicia moved slowly, for her ancient bones permitted no more quick movements. But tonight, tingling with excitement, she almost felt young again.

When the bags were finished, all the Sisters pulled on cloaks. All, except Sister Maria Felicia. The others looked at her with a bit of sadness, for this had been her idea.

"If we walk slowly, perhaps you could come?" one young Sister gently asked.

Laying a veined hand on the young nun's shoulder, Sister Maria Felicia said, "No, go ahead. Secret giving can be tricky. You may have to run. I'd get caught for sure! Go on, now. I'll hear all about it in the morning."

She watched them leave, their arms laden with the bright bags that betrayed their contents by the delicious fragrance. The excited chatter quieted, for all must be silent now.

As they disappeared into the darkness, Sister Maria Felicia stood in the doorway for a moment thinking of the children who would be so surprised in the morning. It would have been nice to go.

But, she must not linger. She had her own secrets!

As quickly as her legs could carry her, Sister Maria Felicia went to the kitchen, and pulled a large tray of small cakes from its hiding place. Oh, the cakes were even more beautiful now than when she had so tiredly finished them in the early hours of this morning!

And now, despite lack of sleep, despite old bones that wouldn't hurry, Sister Maria Felicia began her own journey of surprises, leaving little cakes in places she knew each Sister would surely discover in the morning.

Happily tired, she tumbled into bed, wondering if St. Nicholas had felt this same mixture of excitement and exhaustion after one of his secret journeys. She was asleep in minutes.

Sister Maria Felicia slept so soundly that she never heard the soft footsteps in the hallway, nor heard a basket filled with sweets being placed outside her door.

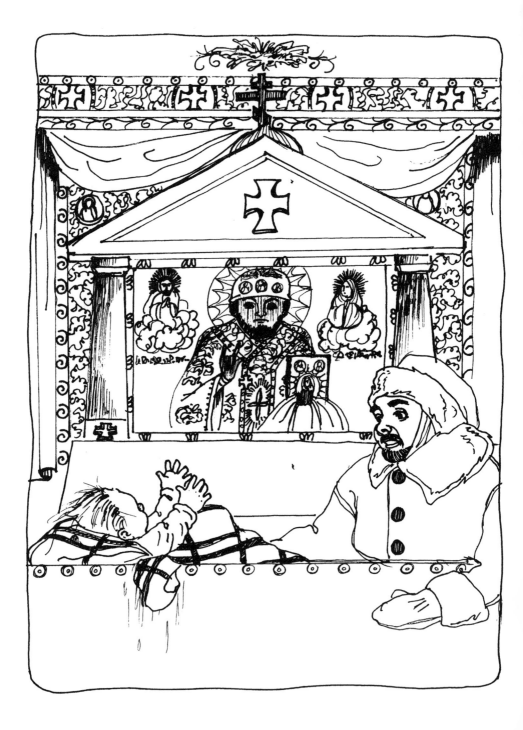

12

A Tale from Russia: Nikolai Chudovorits

St. Nicholas was loved and honored in many countries, and had an especially strong following in Russia, when Christianity spread there in the eighth century. It was said that there were few villages that did not claim a miracle performed by him. Stories abound of his intercession there, such as his freeing an innocent prisoner, and of helping an impoverished merchant by buying his goods and returning them to the merchant's wife. Among the most dramatic are tales of children being saved by the good saint. This is one of them.

The baby had been restless all during church. Katya was weary of struggling with him during the long service, and now, as they approached the bridge, her arms ached.

"Do you want me to hold him?" Pyotr, her husband, offered.

"No," she answered. "I want to wrap him in my shawl while we go over the bridge. It's so much colder up there."

"Little Ivan," said Pyotr affectionately, patting the baby. "You are so anxious to walk! What is your hurry? After you learn, you must walk the rest of your life!"

"My mother says he is just like my younger brother. Some babies just seem to have a drive to walk. She says they run before they walk."

Despite her weariness, Katya smiled. She liked the idea of this lively firstborn being like her brother.

The baby resisted the shawl. He wanted to get down, to crawl in his quick manner. They began walking over the narrow bridge that spanned the River Dnieper. "The river runs especially quickly today," Pyotr commented.

Ivan began to cry, to scream in frustration. He arched his back, and pushed against Katya. He pushed again, and tired Katya could fight back no longer. He slipped from her arms.

She screamed, the baby screamed, Pyotr screamed. The baby was gone! She and Pyotr saw Ivan's little white cap bob in the water below. And then they saw him no more.

Pyotr ran off the bridge, shouting for help, running toward the river, its swift course taking his hopes and dreams away. Others on the street came running, and everyone tried to help. But Ivan was gone.

Katya sat on the bridge, horror filling her. Below her, people shouted as they ran downriver. Her shawl lay limply on the bridge. "Oh, dear God," she prayed. "Help my baby! Help my baby!"

From deep within her, a sob began. Katya cried uncontrollably until Pyotr came for her, his face ashen.

"Let us go home," he said quietly. "The only thing left to do now is to pray. A man told me to pray to the good bishop St. Nicholas. He has saved children before. You know, he is called Nikolai Chudovorits."

Katya nodded numbly. "Nicholas the Wonder Worker," she said faintly.

He helped her up. Katya picked up the shawl. Silently, she dropped the shawl over the bridge. They walked home, Katya's sobs the only sound between them.

At home, Pyotr lit a candle and began praying. He did not eat. He prayed, asking Nikolai Chudovorits to perform a wonder now and bring little Ivan back to them.

Neighbors came to console. As Katya cried, Pyotr prayed. Family members rushed to the little house. Katya sobbed, and Pyotr prayed. The grandmothers stayed with them all night, holding Katya, crying among themselves.

74

Pyotr did not sleep. He ate a little soup, then went back to prayer. That is how they spent the night.

Gray dawn arrived, and with it, the young man who worked at the Cathedral of St. Sofia set out in the chill for his morning duties. Entering the dark building, he saw only the flickering soft lights of the candles. But what was that sound? He stopped.

A baby? A baby crying! Right here, within the cathedral, he heard a baby crying. Why would someone be here this early with a baby, he wondered. And how would they have gotten in? He had unlocked the great doors! But there was no doubt that a baby was here, a hungry one at that, the man thought. He would have to investigate.

The sound came from the place where the painting, the icon, of St. Nicholas, stood. He hurried there. Under the icon lay a baby, wrapped in a shawl, dressed in what had been warm clothing. But the baby was soaking wet, from head to toe, as if he had been swimming.

He thought of the story he'd heard about the baby that had drowned the day before. He picked up the crying child, despite its wet clothing. Then he looked up into the face of the painting, and he understood.

He began to shout, over the baby's cries. "It was Nikolai Chudovorits! It is a miracle! The child lives!"

Running from the cathedral with the baby in his arms, he continued to shout, "It is a miracle! We must find the parents! St. Nicholas has restored their child!"

A passerby stopped to listen, stopped to look.

"Why, this is Pyotr and Katya's child! Here! Alive!" he marveled. "Praise God! Thank God!"

"Run and tell the parents!"

And he ran off to their home, where Pyotr was still praying.

13

A Tale from Germany: King in the Choir, Apples in the Aisle

In England, the pagan winter celebration included a turnabout time, when the powerful changed places with the lowly in riotous festivities. These celebrations were echoed in the tenth to sixteenth centuries with the "Boy Bishop" traditions that spread across France, Germany, the Netherlands, Belgium, and Switzerland as well as England. Commemorating St. Nicholas's appointment to bishop at a young age, the merrymaking provided much fun for children and adults alike. This story is based on records from Germany that tell of a king taking special delight in the frolics one year.

"Boys!" whispered the choirmaster. "I have incredible news! The king is coming!"

"Our king, Father? The king? King Conrad?" came the astounded whispered questions.

"Yes! He's heard of our Boy Bishop tradition and has come to watch," the choirmaster explained.

"When, Father?" Karl asked.

"This very minute! Act your parts, and have fun!" he said, and then hurried down the side aisle to the choir stalls.

The choirboys stared at one another. The king! This was more unbelievable than what was already happening! But the music had begun and they each had parts to play, king or no king.

For this was St. Nicholas Day, the day when the priests of his church chose a boy to become bishop for a month.

During this month, everything was turned around: the powerful were made lowly, the lowly were powerful, the playful were serious, the serious ones could be silly.

Karl had never expected to be chosen Boy Bishop, but here he was, standing in the shadowy vestibule of the monastery church, a bishop's jeweled hat, the miter, on his head. Rich vestments covered his shoulders, silver and gold rings glinted from his fingers. The other boys were dressed as priests.

They lined up for the procession into the church, all very serious. Each hoped for a glimpse of the king, not one daring to look around. They were the adults today.

Karl, last in the procession, straightened his robes, lifted his mitered head high, and began his stately walk down the aisle. He, too, resisted the urge to look about. No bishop would do such an irreverent thing.

His heart pounded. This was only the beginning. For a month, he would be bishop, in remembrance of St. Nicholas becoming a bishop as a very young man. As bishop, Karl would attend dinners given in his honor, preside at more church services, and collect money for the church.

His friends in front of him were walking in ceremonious procession, which the priests did in ordinary times. Karl knew from other years that no boy ever disgraced the others by acting like a child.

But it was not easy, for the real adults, always so serious, often stern, forever dignified and formal, became children for this short time. And their antics were often more outrageous than those of any real child.

Just as Karl felt he had gotten used to walking smoothly despite his splendid clothing, he realized that the choirmaster was now dressed in ragged clothing. On his nose were spectacles made of orange peels! Other priests, dressed in as silly a manner, were jeering at him. Two others were dancing to the music!

Quickly Karl looked away. He must not laugh. He was the bishop.

He had reached the front of the church, and now it was time to take the lead. Karl stepped forward to begin the prayer, only to realize that a priest was riding a toy horse down the center aisle!

Karl raised his eyes heavenward, knowing a bishop would, but also that it would keep him from laughing. He said the words of the prayer with all the seriousness a bishop could muster.

The bespectacled choirmaster began a hymn. All the members of his choir held their books upside down! And instead of the music they had sung earlier, a crashing and tootling filled the church as they played pipes and drums!

When the racket quieted, Karl faced his hardest moment, for he must give a sermon. Walking slowly so his miter would not topple, Karl stepped into the pulpit. Would anyone listen to the words he had written?

Karl heard a noise, a sound he could not identify, a very unchurch-like sound. Confused, he paused. And then he saw: apples. Apples were rolling down the aisle! Someone in the back of the church was flinging fruit!

Priests in other seats clapped and laughed, whistled and made faces.

Karl closed his eyes for a moment to remember his words. He opened them, and began speaking over the sound of rolling apples. Then he gave a small start, for there was the king!

King Conrad was sitting with the unruly choir members and laughing with abandon!

Once more, Karl began, and this time was able to

complete the sermon. He blessed everyone, and then, with solemnity, Karl and his priests walked down the apple-strewn aisle, as the silly music accompanied them.

When the boys reached the back of the church, the king joined them, delight in his face and words of praise and congratulations on his lips.

Karl, the Boy Bishop, knew the real Bishop Nicholas would have greeted rulers with respect and grace. Karl did so now.

14

A Tale from Siberia: Smoke in the Darkness

The reindeer people of Siberia, family groups who made their living herding reindeer, had a rich spirituality. It included a holy man who traveled by magic reindeer, and entered snow-covered winter homes through the smoke hole in the roof. When Christian missionaries ventured as far north as the Arctic Circle in the seventeenth century, they brought with them stories of St. Nicholas as part of their teachings of Christ. Often, a people's tradition and Christianity were combined in ways that fit both religions' symbolisms. It may be that our modern-day Santa Claus comes down chimneys and drives a sleigh pulled by flying reindeer because of these two cultures coming together.

In the following story, children can see a glimpse of the reindeer people's religious views. They can also see a bit of Christianity from the perspective of someone hearing about it for the first time.

Lopahin snuggled on the bed, a pile of reindeer hides that lay as close to the fire as safety would allow. It was dark. It was always dark, it seemed, in the wintertime. His mother, father, and grandmother sat near the fire with the uncle who was talking quietly so the child could go to sleep.

Outside, the wind howled. Lopahin could hear the hard, biting snow pelting the timber walls. And the darkness was all around, except for the orange glow from the fire. Sleepy, but not yet asleep, he watched the smoke curl around, then find its way to the main opening in the house, the smoke hole in the roof. The smoke escaped through the hole, to who-knows-where. The child didn't know. It was so long since he had left this little house. So long since it was light, and summer, so long since they lived in a tent and followed the hundreds of reindeer his family herded.

Sleep had almost overtaken him when his uncle's voice rose, just a little.

"I met two men that have come from far away. They're from warm places, but they have come all this way here to talk with us about our holy man," his uncle said.

Lopahin did not move, lest they see he was still awake and stop talking altogether. But he listened, for he loved to hear stories of the Holy Man, the shaman.

"I told them of the shaman, how we call him when someone is sick or dying. I said that life was like a tree — the roots are underground, in the world of the dead, and the branches reach the heavens. The trunk in between is the earth. Sometimes, if we need to connect with the heavens, the shaman can help."

Lopahin loved that story. His grandmother had told it to him, while his father carved notches in the big pole in the center of the house, to show Lopahin the way life was like a tree.

"The men asked how our shaman is able to travel when it gets so cold. I told him of the shaman's helpers," the uncle went on.

The others nodded. In the darkness, Lopahin nodded, too. He knew the helpers. One was a bird, which guided the shaman to the upper world. The next was a fish that took him to the underworld. And lastly, the magic reindeer, who protected the shaman. This was Lopahin's favorite. He saw reindeer all the time, hundreds of reindeer; but this one, he knew, was special. He loved to imagine a reindeer that could protect him. Would it look different from the regular reindeer? What magic could it do?

His uncle went on.

"Then the strangers said they'd tell me about their God-man. They call him Jesus. They said there was much to tell of this Jesus. The God-man has some holy people like our shaman. One holy man is named Nicholas. This Nicholas travels to help people. He has cured people, like our shaman. I asked the stranger many more questions. He'll come in the spring, before we leave, to tell us more, about this God-man, Jesus, and his shaman, Nicholas. . . ."

Lopahin stirred under the comfort of the blankets, saw a wisp of smoke rise through the hole once more, wondered about all he had heard. He hoped he'd hear more in the spring. But right now, he was so sleepy and his bed was so comfortable. The wind hurled snow against the walls of his safe house. Closing his eyes, Lopahin fell asleep.

15

A Tale from Greece: The Sun on the Sea

Greece is known for its numerous monasteries, some of which are perched on remote mountainsides. One monastery, dedicated to St. Nicholas, was home to a painting of him that was known as a "wonder-working icon." Each year, in a festival held there, thousands would come to honor the icon. Interestingly, this festival coincided with the Bari festival days, which commemorated the arrival of Nicholas's remains in Bari.

The following story, from 1909, tells of a miracle attributed to St. Nicholas that occurred during these holy days in the monastery.

Kyriakula sat on the sun-warmed bench. Far below, she could hear the restlessness of the sea. The wind blew constantly, tangling her long, black hair. She listened to the silence, knowing that in a few days this serene place would be filled with pilgrims. People like herself would come to ask St. Nicholas a special favor.

She sat in the middle of the monastery courtyard, having finished eating earlier than her father. He would come for her soon, and then they would go into the church to pray. Kyriakula wanted to be outside in the wind and sun as long as she could.

When they first arrived, her father had described the monastery to her. Some of the rooms were graced with detailed paintings of saints, angels, and of Christ himself. With words, he had shown her colors, the expressions on faces, the number of the paintings, so she could imagine the beauty of this place. Kyriakula had listened to these words, but she had heard something else, too. She had heard her father's sorrow at her blindness. And she heard his hope that in coming to this monastery dedicated to St. Nicholas, she would be blessed by the saint, and regain her sight.

She knew she must pray with her father, if only to keep from disappointing him. He had left his farmwork behind, something he rarely could do. He had left the rest of the family behind, to travel all this way for her. It had been a long journey from their village, but he had led her, had helped her, and told her of the beauty surrounding them all the way.

They would begin to pray as soon as he had finished his meal and had come for her. It was Wednesday, and by Friday, others would arrive for the festival that would be celebrated on Saturday. Her father wanted to come a few days early to pray. Did she think her father expected a miracle? Kyriakula did not know. St. Nicholas could do great things. But did miracles happen now? After all, this was 1909. "This was not an age of miracles," she had heard a neighbor tell her father.

Footsteps approached her. Her father's voice was cheerful, "I'm here. Let's go into the church."

It was cool inside, and Kyriakula liked the smell that greeted her. Her father led her to a place that she imagined held the holy icon, a painting of St. Nicholas. They prayed there for the rest of the day.

On Thursday, Kyriakula longed to be outside, not in the church, but she did not complain. Her father prayed continually, and she did her best to follow his example.

As the day of the festival approached, more and more people arrived at the monastery. A number of others joined

Kyriakula and her father in silent meditation in the church.

Saturday was the day of the festival. At dawn, Kyriakula felt the presence of a full church, though all were silent, deep in prayer.

Then something changed. Kyriakula felt a strange sensation she had no words for. What was happening?

She jerked her head up swiftly. Had she fallen asleep? Was she dreaming that she saw light again? No, she was awake! Faster and faster, light was returning to her eyes! Kyriakula jumped to her feet.

"Father!" she cried out in the silence of the church. "Father, I can see! I can see!"

She whirled about, with the grace of one who knows where she is going.

"There are the candles! There is the painting, the icon of St. Nicholas! I can see them! I can see it all!"

Startled, her father stood up, staring at her dumbly. Then, understanding, he flung his arms around her. Kyriakula felt his tears fall on her hair.

Others near her began exclaiming, "The child sees! It is a miracle!"

Joy and excitement spread throughout the crowded church. Many came up to Kyriakula and stroked her hair, congratulating her. Some cried, others shouted St. Nicholas's praises loudly. And then, they quieted again, to give thanks for this miracle. Kyriakula wanted to run because she could see to run. She wanted to see the sea, and the paintings. But that must wait. Thanksgiving was more important. So, she focused on the icon, and tried to say how grateful she was, how thankful she would always be.

At the festival later that day, she looked hungrily at the

water, at the paintings, at the people, at the food, and most of all, at her father, whose face was shining like the sun on the sea.

And when it was time to go home, Kyriakula did not need her father's guidance. She led the way, a miracle for all her world to see.

16

A Tale from Belgium:
A Wartime Visit

In 1916, when the world was in the midst of the first terrible world war, a group of Belgian refugee children learned that despite the ravages of war, the spirit of giving and surprise continues. Centuries after St. Nicholas lived, the survival of that spirit is a gift we still receive from the holy bishop of long ago.

Mireille tucked her doll into bed. The doll had been kissed so many times that her forehead and cheeks were stained. Yet, she still wore her blue dress trimmed with the beautiful lace Grandmama had made long ago. Kissing the doll once again, Mireille tenderly slid her into the tattered box she called a bed, and said good night.

"Mireille," a voice called softly.

She looked up into the gentle smile of her older brother, Denis.

"Here. Have my bread," he said, squatting down to hand her the roll from his supper as if it were a fine gift.

"Why?"

"Because it is the only gift I can give you."

"Thank you," Mireille said, taking the bread. Food was not plentiful. "But why give me a gift?"

He smiled again. Mireille suddenly remembered that Grandmama always said Denis's smile was like the sun coming out after a thunderstorm.

"Silly kid. Don't you know what day it is?"

She shook her head.

"December fifth. St. Nicholas Eve."

"Oh!" Mireille jumped up, clapping her hands. "St. Nicholas! Oh, yes! He will come tonight!"

"Hush!" Denis said. "No, he won't. He can't. That's why I want you to have my bread. I know it's nothing, but at least you can say you got a surprise on St. Nicholas Eve!"

Mireille stopped clapping. "What do you mean he won't come?"

"Oh, Mirie, this is war! Our country has been taken over by another! We have been sent away from home so we will be safe. Do you really think St. Nicholas can come and find us?"

"Yes! Yes, he will!" Mireille said hotly.

"Then I'm sorry I reminded you. I'd heard other kids talking about it, so I figured you'd remember. Don't expect him, Mireille. War changes all things," Denis said, sounding maddeningly like a grown-up. He stood up. "I'm going outside to play while there is still light."

Mireille looked at the roll in her hand, then at her doll. Breaking the bread in half, she stuffed one part into her mouth. Tenderly, she placed the other into the doll's hand.

"Happy St. Nicholas Eve," she whispered. "Maybe Denis will be wrong. He's not always right, you know."

Mireille walked to the door. Outside, in the December cold, many children played and jumped and shouted. Denis and some other big boys were throwing a ball and scrambling for it in some game Mireille did not understand.

She shivered.

If only she could go home, back to Belgium, where St. Nicholas could come for sure. Two years earlier, soldiers had arrived, demanding to cross into Belgium. King Albert, Belgium's tall, handsome leader, had said no. He declared that Belgium would fight, even though their country had never fought in a war before. And, Mireille knew, the

Belgian soldiers had fought bravely. But there were so many other soldiers, too many others. Soon, Belgium had been defeated. Later, Mireille and Denis and other children had been sent to Varengeville-sur-Mer, in France, to be safe. Here they remained as the war raged on. If only she could go back to Liège, her city, where St. Nicholas was a patron saint. Maybe there, even with the war, he could come.

She should be a brave Belgian, like King Albert and the soldiers. But she felt no bravery today. She only felt cold, and a long way from home.

Clang, clang! Mireille looked around, and others stopped their play, too. She heard the sound again. It was a bell, a handbell. What could it mean? From around a corner came a man. He was dressed in a long, beautiful red cloak and he carried a bishop's staff.

"St. Nicholas!" Mireille cried. "I knew you'd come!"

The other children ran to him, shouting, and Mireille joined them. As if they were at home, they knelt down in front of him, and he blessed each one. Next, the children sang for the good saint. As he listened, Mireille saw tears in his eyes.

The song ended, and St. Nicholas said in a loud voice, so all could hear, "Let's go inside, where we can talk about how you have all been. And then, perhaps I have some gifts for you!"

A cheer went up, and other children rushed ahead. Mireille waited, hoping to walk with him.

"I knew you'd come," she said shyly. "Even with the war."

"Then you have great faith, even with the war," the bishop said.

Denis hurried toward them. The bishop looked at him

and said, "I have heard that you are especially kind to your little sister."

Denis looked surprised. But then he smiled. It was as if the sun had come out after a great thunderstorm.

Someday the war would end, Mireille knew. But St. Nicholas would always be.

17

A Tale from the Netherlands: Sinterklaas

Today, St. Nicholas has a whole season unto himself in the Nether-
lands. Weeks before his December sixth feast day, he officially arrives
in the Netherlands by steamer, which chugs through the canals with
great ceremony. Welcomed by mayors, followed by television cameras,
and cheered by throngs of Dutch admirers, his entrance into the coun-
try means the season of winter merriment has begun in the Nether-
lands. Dutch children know that once he arrives, St. Nicholas spends
the nights riding over the rooftops on his magnificent white horse,
tossing toys and other gifts down chimneys.

His name shortened to "Sinterklaas," he now plays not a reli-
gious role, but that of a secular spirit of goodness. In the Nether-
lands as well as Belgium, he is loved by Christian, Jewish, and Mus-
lim children alike.

Sinterklaas's ship, the Spanje, *is said to arrive from Spain each*
year. Clad in rich bishop's clothing, Nicholas is accompanied by his
mischievous helper, Zwarte Piet, who is dressed like a sixteenth-cen-
tury page of Moorish descent. Their clothing depicts a time in Dutch
history, beginning in the 1400s, when the Netherlands became a
Spanish possession. Then, all administrators and clergy and some
staff came from Spain, dressed in medieval clothing.

All this matters very little to the excited Dutch children who
know that as that steamer approaches, a time of magic has begun.

"It's truly St. Nicholas weather," said a voice above
Annemie.

She shivered and looked up. Pressed in by a crowd of
winter-coated adults, she could only see the cheerless gray
sky.

"Yes," she heard her father agree. "The drearier it is, the more *gezeling!*"

Her father meant warm and cozy, Annemie knew, thinking of how delightfully warm her home would be when they went back there. But she would not go home right now for anything.

She shivered again, with excitement this time. For today was the day that St. Nicholas, Sinterklaas, would arrive! Throngs of people lined the streets of Amsterdam, waiting to see him. Flags fluttered from houses, and balloons bobbed everywhere. Annemie, her family, and hundreds of others had been waiting here for hours.

A booming sound broke through the crowd noise, and everyone perked up. Then the air was filled with the bonging, chiming, and tolling of many church bells.

"There's the ship!" Annemie's father shouted. "Here comes the *Spanje!* Here, Annemie, get onto my shoulders. I don't want you to miss a thing!"

Her older sister, Sofie, clung to a railing of some nearby steps. Their mother stood with her. Within seconds, Annemie sat astride her father's sturdy shoulders. In the distance, coming up the channel, was the steamship.

"I see him!" her father called up to her. "Can you see Sinterklaas?"

Annemie couldn't answer. She could only look. At the helm of the *Spanje* stood a magnificent figure, a tall man with a long white beard Annemie longed to touch. He was made even taller by the red miter, the bishop's hat that perched on his head. He wore a white robe, whose cuffs were edged in inches of lace. Over that was his famous red cloak that looked almost as soft as his beard. Annemie gazed longingly at this man as his ship came closer and closer.

Around her, people were cheering. Sofie clapped and shouted, "There's Zwarte Piet!"

Yes, Annemie noticed. There was Zwarte Piet, Sinterklaas's helper. In fact, there were many Zwarte Piets, many helpers. They were all dressed in bright colors, with balloonlike short pants and stockings similar to Annemie's tights. Sofie loved Zwarte Piet, for he was always silly, always up to tricks. And, she knew, his bag was filled with treats. But Annemie looked back to Sinterklaas. He was waving. Perhaps he was waving just to her. She put up one mittened hand, and waved back.

The ship had stopped, and the television crews moved in, focusing on the *Spanje*. A brass band began playing, the church bells rang continually, the guns kept blasting. All around her, people shouted and cheered. Annemie made not a sound, but her eyes followed the stately bishop's movements as he walked down the plank from the ship.

One Zwarte Piet followed, already making a silly face. Then a beautiful white horse appeared at the plank, and was led down by another Zwarte Piet. Annemie wondered, as she did each year, why the wonderful horse had no name. But Sofie was jumping up and down, hoping for a visit from Zwarte Piet.

The parade began to form. As soon as Sinterklaas mounted his horse, the parade started, the band playing, with uniformed policemen on horseback, acrobats, magnificent floats decorated with scenes from fairy tales, and groups of children.

All the Zwarte Piets began to move into the crowd, but never far from the good Sinterklaas. One approached Sofie, and she squealed as he did a flip near her, despite the closeness of the crowd. Then he asked her to sing a song, and she and other children obliged.

"Good Sinterklaas is in Holland once again, with his horse and Piet from sunny Spain, . . ." they sang.

He clapped and began throwing cookies, oranges, and chocolates into the crowd. Sofie caught several, but Annemie did not try. A bit afraid of Piet's outgoing silliness, she hoped he wouldn't notice her.

But he did. He winked at her. Quick as that wink, Annemie buried her face into her father's hair. She heard and felt her father laugh.

When she looked up, Annemie gasped. The white horse was in front of her! Close enough so that she could touch him was the good saint himself!

"Oh!" she whispered.

The velvet robe flowed in the wind and brushed her knee. Sinterklaas was gazing at her! His eyes kind, his face patient, Sinterklaas knew about shy children.

"Hello," he said, and held out a gloved hand. She was afraid to take it. "You have been good this year!"

Annemie nodded.

"And will you leave some carrots for my horse this year?"

Annemie nodded. And then, she reached out. His gloved hand engulfed hers. He reached with his other hand and touched her cheek. Taking a deep breath, Annemie reached up, and touched that wonderful, fluffy white beard. Sinterklaas smiled.

And then, he moved on.

"Well, what did you think of that, my Annemie?" her father called up to her.

Annemie sighed a big, contented sigh.

As Sinterklaas moved down the street, surrounded by children, Annemie knew he would stop later by the palace and be welcomed by the mayor. Then he would give a little speech, and then many others would clap and cheer. But she wanted to go home.

All the way back to their house, Annemie and Sofie skipped like Zwarte Piet and sang together:

Good Sinterklaas is in Holland again,
With his horse and Piet from sunny Spain.
And even if he can't stay long,
We hope he'll stop to hear our song.
Dear Sinterklaas, the door is open wide,
For you and Piet to step inside.
And we're singing, voices ringing,
And our hearts rejoice
'Cause the saint loves all good girls and boys.

And oh, how warm and cozy was their home when the tired and cold family stepped inside. Annemie took off her coat and went straight into the kitchen, to look for the biggest, juiciest carrot she could find.

Maybe tonight was the night he would pass over her house.

18

A Tale from the United States: The Teddy Bear's Journey

In the United States today, most children do not wait on the fifth of December for the visit of a tall, thin bishop. Instead, they are surrounded by images of a jolly fat man whose mysterious arrival is on Christmas. How did St. Nicholas become Santa Claus?

During the Protestant Reformation, interest in saints declined sharply. In countries that became Protestant, customs of gift giving surrounding St. Nicholas were replaced with other practices, which included new figures, with St. Nicholas-like traits but with new names. Instead of having gifts arrive on St. Nicholas Eve, traditions changed to Christmas Eve. However, in Holland, St. Nicholas remained a constant figure, as sailors of that seafaring nation believed strongly in his protection.

Around 1624, Dutch settlers founded a colony in the New World, the capital called New Amsterdam. Children of Dutch parents were brought up with a belief in St. Nicholas, or as he was called then, Sinter Claes. A ship arrived in New Amsterdam from the Netherlands each year around December fifth, laden with toys, candies, and books for these children, and parties with an appearance by the good saint marked the season leading to Christmas.

When the British seized New Amsterdam (renaming it New York), they brought with them their own customs. English children believed in Father Christmas, who arrived on Christmas Eve. Eventually, citizens of Dutch and English descents married, and customs of Sinter Claes and Father Christmas blended. By the late 1700s, he had an American name: Santa Claus, and he brought gifts on Christmas Eve.

In 1809, author Washington Irving wrote a humorous book chronicling the history of New York. In it, he mentioned the Dutch St. Nicholas traditions, fabricating some of it. Readers took this for fact, and St. Nicholas became more widely known in the young country. Then, one Christmas Eve in 1822, a college professor by the name of Clement Clarke Moore wrote a poem to amuse his wife and children that night. He described Santa Claus as a short, chubby man with a long white beard, having been inspired by an acquaintance with similar features. The poem, now commonly known as " 'Twas The Night Before Christmas" had a profound effect on who Santa became in the United States.

Through newspaper cartoons and commercials, Santa's story evolved further, and now, Santa Claus lives at the North Pole. However, he is very accessible to American children through public appearances and various media. His reputation has been touched by commercialism as his image is borrowed to sell a myriad of products at Christmastime. But this need not diminish his true spirit. Santa is the descendant of St. Nicholas. At his core is still a love of children, a tremendous generosity, an unquestionable kindness, and a propensity for surprises. St. Nicholas's spirit works through the image of Santa Claus. More importantly, the spirit of St. Nicholas is alive and strong within ordinary people who also love children, who are generous and kind, and who still love surprises.

In many parts of the United States, vast programs are organized each Christmas to collect toys for disadvantaged children. Thousands of people buy gifts and deposit them anonymously at drop-off sites, where volunteers collect, sort, and help distribute them in the weeks just before Christmas. While these scenes are drastically different from St. Nicholas's nighttime capers, the motivations are the same.

Across thousands of miles, across major cultural differences, across hundreds of years, the spirit of St. Nicholas lives on in the generosity and anonymity of these gift givers.

"Oh, Daddy! Look! That's just what I want!" said Martin, jumping up and down in the toy aisle. He was pointing at a display of action figures.

"For you or to give to other children?" Daddy asked.

"For me! I want that one!" Martin insisted.

"Martin, we are here to buy gifts for others. Christmas is coming and you'll be getting surprises. But we must help someone who won't have any surprises unless we help. Remember?"

Martin sighed.

"What did you want to pick out with your own money?" Daddy asked.

"A teddy bear."

"Then let's go choose it," Daddy said and hustled Martin away from the tempting figures.

In the stuffed animal aisle, Martin searched carefully. Finally he chose a dark brown bear wearing flannel pajamas.

"It's not too big, and not too little, and it's just right for sleeping with," Martin said, hugging it.

At the checkout, Martin laid his dollars on the counter and watched his money be whisked away. Then he and Daddy placed the bear into a large box labeled "Toys for Donation."

"It's a nice bear," Martin said wistfully.

"It's a great bear. Someone is going to sleep happier because of you, Martin."

"Who?"

"We don't know. We are giving in secret."

Martin was silent as he patted the bear. He left the store reluctantly.

All night, the bear sat in the box. In the morning it was scooped out, and placed into a bag with other toys. Later, this bag was loaded onto a tractor-trailer rig, a huge truck, already filled with toys, and driven to a community center.

There a little girl named Nieves and her *abuelo*, her grandfather, were waiting in the frosty afternoon as the sun sank in the December sky. Along with many other volunteers, they would unload the toys from the truck, and then sort them so the toys could be given away.

As the long truck labored to back into the driveway, *Abuelo* squeezed his granddaughter's hand three times. Nieves smiled up at him and squeezed back three times: I love you.

The truck stopped; the volunteers crowded around. When the back door of the tractor-trailer rig was raised, there were sighs and exclamations from the volunteers.

"Wow! There are even more toys than last year!"

"I've never seen so many toys!"

Abuelo said, "The generosity of people!"

Nieves stared at the truck from the front all the way to the back; from the floor to the ceiling, toys were stuffed, stacked, and packed.

"Let's form a chain and get these inside! It's cold out here!" someone shouted.

Nieves watched as the adults formed a line. Two men climbed onto the truck and began handing bags down to the people on the ground. The bags were passed from person to person, until each bag was placed in the building.

Stiff with cold, the volunteers drank coffee and cocoa gratefully and blew on fingers to warm up. Then the sorting began. There were hockey sticks, basketballs, baby dolls, games, plastic horses, puzzles, balls, baseball gloves, radios, hair dryers, stuffed animals, fashion dolls, video games, building blocks, and boxes of books.

Each volunteer was assigned a category. *Abuelo* and Nieves got stuffed animals. As each bag was unpacked, they found all the bunnies, pandas, dogs, and teddy bears and placed them on a separate table. The helpers were cheerful, and someone put on a tape of Christmas carols. Nieves felt the excitement of Christmas flutter within her. *Abuelo* had said she would like helping.

Then she saw it. It was the cuddliest teddy bear, wearing sweet flannel pajamas. Nieves picked it up and hugged it. She stopped her work, and held it close.

"*Abuelo*? Couldn't I take this home?" she asked delicately.

"No," *Abuelo* said, concentrating on his sorting.

"Couldn't I just take this one toy, for helping?" Nieves wheedled.

He stopped and looked at Nieves hugging the bear. Gently he said, "No. We're here to help, to give of ourselves today. It is not our time for receiving."

Nieves sighed. She gave the teddy one last hug, and placed it on the stuffed-animal table.

After many hours, the toys were all sorted. Nieves, *Abuelo*, and the others left the community center. The lights were turned out, and doors locked. All night, the teddy bear waited on the table with the other stuffed animals.

The next morning dawned gray with a sense of snow in the air, but the center was full of activity. Hopeful parents lined up, waiting to get presents to delight their children, gifts they could not afford to buy.

A young woman approached the stuffed animal table. "Oh, this teddy will be perfect for my baby!" she whispered. Picking up the pajamaed bear, she hugged it.

The bear was placed in a bag and the mother carried it home, to be hidden until Christmas. She smiled with anticipation at seeing her toddler's face on Christmas morning.

That evening, as Nieves snuggled into her warm bed, *Abuelo* quietly left the house. A light snow was falling as he hurried to a toy store, where he quickly found a teddy bear. It was the furriest, cuddliest one on the shelf. Just as the store was closing, *Abuelo* stepped out into the snow, the bear in a bag. Humming to himself, he savored the thought of Christmas Eve when he would surprise Nieves with this bear.

As the snow began to fall more thickly, Martin snuggled in his father's lap at their house.

"I wish I had that teddy bear," Martin said. "The one with the pajamas."

"Let me tell you a story," Daddy said. "Long, long ago, in a land called Asia Minor, there lived a young man named Nicholas. Nicholas loved to use his money to help people, and he often gave gifts to others, but he always gave in secret."

"Like me? With the teddy bear?" Martin asked, sitting up.

"Like you, Martin. Now one day, Nicholas heard about three sisters who needed money badly. So Nicholas waited until late at night, and ducked outside. Very quietly, he crept to their house. Then, quickly, he dropped a bag of gold into the window!"

"A teddy bear would have been quieter," Martin observed.

Daddy laughed, and then went on, "In the morning, the sisters found the gold — "

"On Christmas, will somebody find the teddy bear at their house?"

"Yes, Martin."

Martin lay back down against his father's chest. "I bet they'll be happy," Martin said, and he smiled.

Epilogue: The Spirit Within

The fifth of December is not a major holiday in the United States as it is in the Netherlands, but we can celebrate the spirit of St. Nicholas within us. Our celebrations can range from very simple to elaborate.

At my house, out comes the Christmas tablecloth, replacing the Advent one for this one night. Candles, the good dishes, and our large and delightfully diverse collection of St. Nicholas figures grace the dinner table. We have a special meal that concludes with tea and cake, and the children place shoes by the fireplace for St. Nicholas to fill during the night.

We have celebrated in other ways, too. Here are some suggestions that can be used in a variety of settings:

AT HOME:

❋ Use this book for family reading during Advent, starting on St. Nicholas Eve.

❋ Host a party in which guests bring toys or medical supplies to be given to children in need. Read stories from this book and have a surprise treat for guests. Someone with a flair for the dramatic could dress as St. Nicholas to hand out the treats.

Before the party, contact places that will accept your donations. Sometimes they will give you suggestions, making the choosing of gifts easier and more fun for your guests. One year, we gave gifts to little ones staying in a shelter for women and children. Other times, we have hosted parties where toys and medicines collected were then sent to orphanages in Korea. One family could offer the party, or several families could work together. This could also be a parish event.

❋ Make some treats, and sneak around to neighbors' or friends' houses, leaving the surprises on doorsteps; or leave a family member a breakfast treat outside a bedroom door. Some traditional St. Nicholas cookies are Pepernoten and Speculaas.

❋ As a family, donate money to a children's charity anonymously.

❋ Choose one of the stories in this book and encourage children to dramatize it with simple stick puppets.

❋ Have a "Boy Bishop" or turnabout day where children and adults trade places for a few hours.

In schools:

❄ Starting several days before St. Nicholas Day, read a story a day. Locate the settings for the stories on a map. Have a special treat, preferably given in secret, to arrive on St. Nicholas Day.

❄ Plan with children how to surprise someone for St. Nicholas Day. Children could make simple art projects to leave as a surprise in a nursing home, in their own homes, or to give to another class. In some classrooms it may be feasible for children to leave small surprises for one another.

❄ Bring in books on Christmas customs around the world (quite common in public libraries). Help children research a variety of customs in the countries mentioned in this book.

❄ Older children could use one of these stories and write it as a play, producing it for the school for St. Nicholas Day, or use the following script, *Midnight Missions*. Centuries ago, schoolchildren in Europe often produced plays about the saint's life in celebration of St. Nicholas Day.

In parishes:

❄ Because his feast day comes at the beginning of Advent, St. Nicholas is an excellent subject for a parish Advent retreat. Learning traditional songs, making surprises that could be taken home to be given to unsuspecting family members or neighbors, and a reading of some of these stories could put many in the spirit of giving as well as anticipation.

❄ St. Nicholas's life exemplified many aspects of Christianity. One of these stories could be used as a homily for a children's Mass.

❄ A "Secret St. Nicholas" program can be organized within a parish (or within a program of the parish, such as a youth group) where parishioners live relatively close. Interested people are asked to sign up, giving names and ages of the people in their household, as well as their address. This information can be placed into a box, and all who have signed up then choose, at random, the information about another household. Then, over the course of Advent, little surprises can be done for the chosen household. Sometime before Epiphany, the identity of the "secret St. Nicholases" could be revealed, on an individual basis, or at a gathering. A group could choose instead not to reveal the gift-givers' identities, just as St. Nicholas did not. However, learning the identity of the givers can be a community builder within a group.

❄ The script *Midnight Missions* could be used in a retreat, in Sunday school programs, and as a homily.

'Midnight Missions':
A Script for a St. Nicholas Day Play

The following is a short, simple play that can be easily produced for home, school, or parish use. It is basically a story-telling tool to introduce St. Nicholas, and can be used for an audience of mixed ages. The only actors needed are a narrator and "St. Nicholas," and props can be minimal or nonexistent.

Narrator:

Hundreds of years ago, in the country we now call Turkey, there lived a wealthy child named Nicholas. He lived around the first half of the fourth century. He became a priest, and soon a bishop. Bishop Nicholas worked for justice among all people, and the name Nicholas means "victory of the people."

He helped those who were poor, and those in danger in his lifetime, and he is said to have accomplished even more after his death!

Nicholas appeared to Emperor Constantine of Rome in a dream to convince him to set some prisoners free. Sailors who nearly drowned in a storm were saved by the good bishop who mysteriously landed on board their sinking ship. When a baby was swept into a swift moving river and all efforts to save him failed, the baby appeared the next day, alive and healthy, in a cathedral, under an icon of St. Nicholas.

He is a saint because he lived what the Gospel asks of us. Because some of his acts were done mysteriously, Nicholas has become our saint of surprises. Now his spirit is within each of us whenever we do a good deed in secret. It seems that his spirit is especially strong at this time of year. So strong, I feel as if he is with us now. . . .

(Enter Nicholas)

Nicholas:

Hello! Greetings, everyone! How are you on this Advent day? Waiting for Christmas? Waiting for the birth of the Christ Child?

Well, I have come to tell you a story, and to ask something of importance of you while you wait.

Once, long, long ago, there was a poor man in my country. I heard the man had a terrible problem. You see, he had three daughters who were all old enough to be married. Way back then, it was a custom for a young woman to bring a gift of money to her new husband when they married. This was called a dowry. But as this man had no money to give his daughters, they could not marry. I'm glad to see that this particular custom has died out!

But then, with no dowry and no marriage, his daughters would have to become slaves! Slaves! Can you imagine the worry this good man and his daughters had?

Well, I had money. My parents had left me more than enough. Of course I would share it with this family.

I knew it would be better if the money were given in secret. So, I took a bag of gold and slipped out into the night. I wore a long cloak with a hood so no one could recognize me. I walked quietly through the streets. It was dark. We did not have streetlights then, you know. Still I walked close to the buildings and kept very quiet — I wanted no one to notice me.

When I reached the house, all was dark and silent. I dared not leave a bag of gold on the doorstep for it would surely be stolen. I had no choice but to slip the bag through the window. As soon as I heard that satisfying thud, I hurried off.

I learned that soon after my nighttime travels, the oldest daughter had been married. It was a modest wedding, but her new husband was a good, loving man. One down, two to go.

I didn't want to wait too long for my next secret mission. After all, the second daughter had to be getting nervous. Again I reached the house without being seen. This time, however, I could see a small light, a candle at a bedside, I supposed, and so I had to wait. The wind was chilly and my feet started to ache, but at last the light was snuffed out. I waited another few moments, then slipped the bag of gold through the window. This time, I didn't wait to hear it land.

Again, I heard news of the second daughter's wedding. One more, I told myself. And before long, I found myself hurrying through the darkness to the house, the last bag of gold heavy in my hand. The house was dark, but I approached the window cautiously. After dropping the bag, I turned to leave, but I heard the door open! I hurried as fast as these two feet could carry me. I can tell you that my cape flew behind me!

A shout behind me broke the silence of the night as I rounded a corner. I did not look back, but I could hear that I was being followed by someone faster than I. He came closer, breathing hard, until he grabbed me with such force we both almost tumbled to the ground.

"Please, please," the father gasped — for that was who it was — as he held on to me.

For a moment we both were silent, panting to catch our breath. Then he looked into my face.

"Nicholas! My neighbor Nicholas! It was you!" he exclaimed.

"Sh!" I shushed him. "Don't wake the neighborhood!"

"Thank you! Thank you! How can I ever thank you enough!" he gushed in a hoarse whisper, and then to my horror, he sank to his knees, bowing in front of me.

"Stand up! Please!" I urged, trying to sound commanding in a soft voice. I did not want someone bowing to me!

But he stayed there, saying, "My daughters thank you, I thank you!"

"Please get up!" I pleaded.

He did so, and I went on, "Promise me one thing!"

"Anything, anything, Nicholas, that is within my power! I am so grateful to you!'

"Don't tell anyone that I gave you the money."

"Not even my daughters?"

"No. No one."

"If that is what you want, but — "

"That is what I want," I declared.

So we parted, and the third daughter was married. But the memory of that time stayed with me, and it was not the last time I gave in secret.

Now, I think the father kept his promise, but after my death it seems that someone must have known, for this story has been told about me. I tell it to you now — since it is no longer a secret — because I must ask something of you.

You see, I am a spirit now, a strong spirit, if I must say so myself. To fulfill my earthly work of giving in secret, I need you. Whenever you give in secret, you are filled with my spirit. I call on all of you to be filled with the spirit of surprises and of giving in secret, to carry on my work here. So please become "little Nicholases" and carry on this important task.

And remember two things: keep to the shadows, and have fun!

Bibliography

Barz, Brigitte. *Festivals with Children.* Floris Books (distributed by Gryphon House, Beltsville, Maryland), 1984.

Bear, Jan and Daria Gray. "The Real St. Nicholas." *The Catholic Digest,* December 1993.

Cascio, Michael and Susan E. Leventhal, executive producers. *Santa Claus.* History Television Network Productions, A & E Television Networks: Biography (marketed by New Video Group, 126 Fifth Avenue, New York, NY 10011), 1995.

Coffin, Tristram Potter. *The Book of Christmas Folklore.* New York: Seabury Press, 1973.

Crichton, Robin. *Who Is Santa Claus? The True Story Behind a Living Legend.* Illustrated by Margaret Nisbet. Edinburgh, Scotland: Canongate, 1987.

"Dear Santa." *Good Housekeeping Magazine,* Vol. 219, No. 6, December 1994.

Engleman, Dennis. "Fröhliche Weihnachten! Christmas in Germany." *Liguorian,* December 1995.

Engleman, Dennis. "The Other Christmas Man." *The Family Digest,* November-December 1995.

Engleman, Dennis Eugene. *Santa Claus or Saint Nicholas: What Should You Tell Children?* Norcross, Georgia: Praxis Publishing, 1994.

Giblin, James Cross. *The Truth About Santa Claus.* New York: Thomas Y. Crowell, 1985.

Hausman, Suzanne, illustrator. *Yes, Virginia.* New York: Elizabeth Press, 1972.

Houbler, Dorothy and Thomas. *An Album of World War I.* New York: Franklin Watts, 1976.

Krythe, Maymie R. *All About Christmas.* New York: Harper and Row, 1954.

Leckie, Robert. *The Story of World War I.* Adapted for young readers from the American Heritage History of "World War I" by the Editors of *American Heritage* with narration by S. L. Marshall. New York: Random House, 1965.

McKnight, George H. *St. Nicholas, His Legend and His Role in the Christmas Celebration and Other Popular Customs.* New York: G. P. Putnam's Sons, 1917.

Merin, Jennifer. "For Children in Holland, It's Sinterklaas." *Stevens Point* [Wisc.] *Journal,* November 22, 1995.

Nault, William H., Editorial Director, and Fertig, Theresa Kryst, writer. *Christmas in the Netherlands*. Chicago: World Book-Childcraft International, Inc., a subsidiary of The Scott and Fetzer Company, 1981.

Nelson, Gertrud Mueller. *To Dance With God*. Mahwah, New Jersey: Paulist Press, 1986.

Sherrard, Philip, and the Editors of Time-Life Books. *Byzantium*. New York: Time Incorporated, 1966.

Tilton, Rafael. *The Immortal Dragon of Sylene and Other Faith Tales*. Minneapolis: Winston Press, 1982.

Tschizewskij, Dmitrij. *The Icons of St. Nick*. Translated by Hans Rosenwald. Recklinghausen, Germany: Aurel Bongers Publishers, 1957; Vaduz, Liechtenstein: Overseas Publishers, 1964.

de Voragine, Jacobus. *The Golden Legend, Readings on the Saints*. Vol. 1. Translated by William Granger Ryan. Princeton: Princeton University Press, 1993.

Weil, Lisl. *Santa Claus Around the World*. New York: Holiday House, 1987.

About the Author

This book by Anne E. Neuberger is the latest among several works she has written for children. Her short stories, articles, and award-winning columns appear in various publications.

Neuberger has given numerous workshops to parents, teachers, librarians, and children, and she is a member of the Society of Children's Book Writers and Illustrators (SCBWI).

Before becoming a full-time free-lance writer in 1986, the author was an early-childhood teacher, having earned her BA in this field in 1976. She and her husband are the parents of two boys and two girls.

Our Sunday Visitor. . .

Your Source for Discovering the Riches of the Catholic Faith

Our Sunday Visitor has an extensive line of materials for young children, teens, and adults. Our books, Bibles, booklets, CD-ROMs, audios, and videos are available in bookstores worldwide. To receive a FREE full-line catalog or for more information, call **Our Sunday Visitor** at **1-800-348-2440**. Or write, **Our Sunday Visitor** / 200 Noll Plaza / Huntington, IN 46750.

- -

Please send me: ___A catalog
Please send me materials on:
___Apologetics and catechetics   ___Reference works
___Prayer books   ___Heritage and the saints
___The family   ___The parish

Name_____

Address_____Apt._____

City_____State____Zip_____

Telephone (   ) _____

A09BBABP

- -

Please send a friend: ___A catalog
Please send a friend materials on:
___Apologetics and catechetics   ___Reference works
___Prayer books   ___Heritage and the saints
___The family   ___The parish

Name_____

Address_____Apt._____

City_____State____Zip_____

Telephone (   ) _____

A09BBABP

- -

Our Sunday Visitor
200 Noll Plaza
Huntington, IN 46750
Toll free: 1-800-348-2440
E-mail: osvbooks@osv.com
Website: www.osv.com

Your Source for Discovering the Riches of the Catholic Faith